Top Teacher Tips for Outstar

or

Turning Around Terrible Behaviour

How to have lessons about which all of the following are true:

> ALL the kids in ALL your classes turn up early EVERY LESSON, even when they are at the end of break.
> ALL the kids tell their parents that your lesson is the best lesson, regardless of what subject you teach.
> At the end of EVERY lesson NONE of the kids pack up early or want to go and many ask if they can stay on EVEN when it's the END of the day and many say "What happened to that lesson? Why do the lessons you enjoy go so quickly!"

Introduction
I was a teacher for 34 years. During my career I was, at various times:

> An NQT in a school far from home where the accent was different to my own.
> A young Teacher of History and Archaeology.
> A Drama Teacher.
> A Head of a Drama Department.
> A Head of a large year group with 12 forms.

- ➢ A House Leader with 17 mentors.
- ➢ A Trip Leader of 30+ residential holidays, mostly to Spain and Italy, but including Borneo, Alaska and the Amazon.
- ➢ A Teacher of "Enterprise" at KS3.
- ➢ A Teacher of "Employability Skills and "Business Enterprise" at KS4.
- ➢ A Manager of an Inclusion Unit.
- ➢ A Behaviour Specialist sent to support in a school in Special Measures and desperate trouble.
- ➢ A County AST specialising in Gifted and Talented Education, Cross-phase.
- ➢ A Lead Practitioner in Transition.
- ➢ And lately I have been working as an Education Consultant for a successful MAT.

When I left I received hundreds of cards and messages of goodwill, respect and affection.

For all of the above, I feel qualified to write this short guide. Much of what it contains goes against current training and may be at odds with the policy of the school in which you find yourself.

You will find no names on whiteboards, no ticks and crosses and no detention policy here.

You must decide how much of the advice you want to take, or are able to take.

Each idea alone will help, all together they will make a huge difference, especially if you are in a school where behaviour is poor and "support" from above, ineffective or just not available.

There is no body of research behind this. You will find no references to published practitioners. This is what I did, and it worked.

The Anecdote from which I will draw out the suggested good practice.

Well into my career I was asked to take on the management of the Inclusion Unit in the large mainstream specialist sports college in which I had worked for many years.

18 months into that post I was seconded to a secondary school that was in special measures and desperate trouble. I won't name it.

Shortly after I arrived the Head called an assembly and announced his resignation. The fire alarms were going off daily and there was a county team in place to try and sort things out. A fifth of the staff were NQT's, mostly from abroad. They had a fledgling Inclusion Unit which was actually an Exclusion Unit where unmanageably kids were contained.

Breaks were long, when the staff would retreat to the staffroom to commiserate with each other and be served tea and biscuits.

There was some good teaching going on and any number of caring committed staff. Lessons of "Teachers in Authority" and with several years under their belt were fine, but overall it just wasn't working.

There was a very high percentage of very challenging children, many of whom had already been excluded elsewhere, or who were riding "The County Carousel". {This, for those who don't know, is a counties way of massaging exclusion figures to disguise failure (not theirs, this is a central government issue). Students aren't excluded, they are just moved from school to school on a regular basis until they leave}.

My role was to analyse the problem and suggest solutions whilst working closely with the NQT's.

Inevitably, as a "behaviour expert", I was given the most challenging class in the school in the dingiest classroom for the least popular {in that school} subject, which was Religious Education, and everyone sat back to watch the show.

I'm calling them 8UX. A large mixed-ability group, mostly white British. A scattering of identified special needs. One girl on her third secondary school, one boy on the

Carousel. Maybe six who would have been in a grammar stream if such a thing had existed.

I had them, or they had me, for two fifty-minute periods a week. In my time there, this meant twelve lessons.

Given my seniority at my main school, and my longevity there and my place in the Community I had not experienced personal behaviour issues for a long time, although I managed issues for other staff and students on a daily basis.

I was in for a bit of a shock.

Having viewed the tatty outdated textbooks, I created a beautiful worksheet based on the terms given topic, which was Islam.

The tasks were well structured and differentiated. Everything you would expect from an expert teacher was there. I arrived early for the lesson, laid out my materials, including their books according to my seating plan. Put everything on the board I needed {just an old-fashioned whiteboard back then}. Made sure the classroom was bright and well ventilated and confidently waited, and waited, and waited some more.

Eventually the class turned up. I later learnt that hanging around in the playground for a chat, and even a cigarette, between consecutive lessons was pretty much the standard. With no thought of queueing they bowled in. I was standing by the door ready to greet each one. They behaved as if I did not exist. With one or two exceptions, they picked up my worksheets and either screwed them up and used them as weapons to throw at each other, and me when my back was turned, or they made paper airplanes to project out of the windows. If they sat at all, they sat where they liked, including on the floor under the tables.

I tried waiting, I tried projecting using my best drama teacher's technique, I tried one to one instructions and got;

"Why are you picking on me, look at what he is doing."
"I'll deal with him next, now I'm talking to you."

At which point backs would be turned.
I tried writing on the board something like,

"If you don't stop....." That's as far as I got because a boy removed the pen from my hands and wrote, "F**K OFF, in big letters before throwing the pen out of the window and climbing into a large unlocked cupboard from which he began to throw old models.

Pretty much at the same time the girl who had already been permanently excluded twice got down on the floor and began crawling around under the desks trying to bite the knees of other students, who seemed very used to this.

It was anarchy and nothing I did made any difference at all. By the time I was twenty-five minutes in I had gone through every type of teacher behaviour imaginable, short of physically restraining them, which I wasn't prepared, obviously, to do. At one point, I took a girl out into the corridor to "discuss" her behaviour. The door had a large glass panel. I was surprised that she came with me until I realised that the classroom door was lockable from the inside and that it had, in fact been locked. Fortunately, another student braved the taunting of the others to let me back in.

It became just a containment exercise. They would pause momentarily if I was close by so I just kept moving around to the hotspots until, finally, minutes before the end of the lesson, which preceded lunch, as one they just walked out, with the exception of one boy who stayed behind to help clear up the chaotic mess. In some ways that made it worse because I felt, on top of everything else, that I had failed him as well.

A Teacher in Authority "dropped in" and we discussed my experience. He asked me if I wanted the whole class put in detention. I declined. That has never been my way.

An Adult-Ed group was waiting outside to use the space. The looks on their faces were universally sympathetic. One nice older lady actually said, "You poor man".

Up to that point I had never failed with a class. Even the low-ability year 11's in the ROSLA block doing "European

Studies" in my first term of teaching had been won over. I wasn't about to let this year 8 group be the first.

By the end of lesson 4 they were all on time. They stood in silence for the register, worked hard, were keen to please and left in an orderly file with a smile and a thank you.

The Adult-Ed group actually applauded.

How did I achieve this? The various elements of my plan are the main contents of this book.

Each different idea starts a new page for ease of access.

First, why I don't put names on the board or put children in detention.

Names on the board
I really don't understand what this is all about.

OK. I understand about visually reinforcing good behaviour and reminding them of poor behaviour and also about having escalating consequences BUT

By the time you put their name on the board they have already significantly disrupted the learning. If you go as far as 3 ticks they are clearly not responding. If this happens quickly, where do you go next? If it's the same every lesson, what are you achieving? Clearly nothing except to create a negative atmosphere based on punishment and power.

Detentions
I've only once known a detention do any good. That was with a girl who was persistently late for school, despite always leaving in good time. We'd tried everything else so I agreed with her Dad that until further notice she would complete a full school day whatever time she turned up. Clearly, the fact that she complied shows that she wasn't that difficult but even so, when she was still at her desk at 7.30 pm on the first day of the scheme, it sank in that we meant it. Next day she was on time.

Apart from that detentions are mostly pointless. It's the teacher saying that students have not conformed to the teacher's expectations and so they are going to lose their freedom.

I've seen some appalling practice.

Children "detained" through lunch in an empty classroom whilst the teacher chats in the staffroom.

Children made to stand facing the wall with their nose holding an A4 piece of paper in place.

The same child being in detention every day for the same teachers with no other interventions.

Teachers openly arguing with parents in front of the child, about the detention.

Ask yourself this.

Is it always the same children in detention and does it modify their behaviour? You will find in most cases that the answers are, "yes and no".

This means the system is futile and is more about revenge than building effective teaching and learning relationships.

The basic foundation

It's really all about respect and empathy. That has to work in both directions.

If you only appear at lesson time, fend off personal questions and only ever talk about the work, why shouldn't they think you are a cardboard cut-out who is stored overnight in a cupboard?

Imagine this.

The students who have been annoying you are in control. You are the student. Their curriculum is made up of a study of rap music, skateboarding, YouTubers and Football. That is what you will be made to study in hour long blocks, five a day, five days a week. If you ask to go to the toilet the answer is invariably "NO". At break-time, you are forced outside. At lunchtime, you queue until there is barely time to eat the food you have bought. If you complain or act up in any way, your freedom is taken away. When you go home you are made to write rap songs even though you haven't the first clue how they work and no interest in them whatsoever. If you give up, more of your freedom is taken away.

It's a vision of hell.

It is the reality of school for children who don't want the narrow, middle-class, University driven curriculum that British Schools almost invariably offer. And if they kick off we punish and ultimately exclude them.

Just not good enough.

It also wouldn't be good enough for me to rant on about the failings and inadequacies of that system without offering a practical solution. It will be decades before we move, as a nation, to where we should be, which is pretty much where Finland is now, so my solutions offer a way to work within the current structures that will help you to engage all the students that you work with and to have a positive daily experience of your profession.

Use them all or just the odd one or two. They are described as I applied them to 8UX.

Getting Started

Clearly nothing was achieved in that first lesson. If it continued like that I would not be able to make any progress. To deal with this I unashamedly used the control exerted by that, "Teacher in Authority". He was a House Leader who had been there long enough to teach the parents of these children.

I asked him to come into the start the next lesson for me. They were still late and he told them off for that, which is not what I wanted.
I didn't use the opportunity to verbally attack the class. I used it to tell them something about me, my family, my interests and some anecdotes of the exciting things I had done, mostly around travel and sky-diving.

I then went on to explain to them how their behaviour in the previous lesson had made me feel and that went in with many of them.

I also had a subtext. Carousel Boy, who we'll call Stephen, couldn't actually control himself. His fidgeting turned to open defiance and the TIA removed him. He appeared only briefly in future before being kept away all together. Not ideal, I know, but children operating at this level are not the responsibility of classroom teachers and demand an institutional response.

Other points that I made are better covered elsewhere.

Be in control of your environment

The teaching space was clearly far from ideal. The room didn't have a main teacher using it so the displays were shabby, the cupboards unlockable and full of old, broken work, much of which provided the ammunition during that first lesson. The tables were covered in graffiti, much of it obscene, and, of course, there was that twist lock on the door.

So I went to town, and bought a set of padlocks, a small hacksaw, a roll of bin-liners and a heavy, thick black indelible marker.

First off was the door lock, literally. I sawed it through and threw the twist bit away. Next, I cleared all the accessible surfaces of broken stuff, tatty text books and scraps of paper. Anything which someone might value went in the cupboards, everything else was consigned to the bin-liners. The cupboards were then locked with the padlocks. Having achieved a basic level of clean and tidy I went from desk to desk and blocked out any offensive graffiti.

Now it was the turn of the displays. Anything old and tatty was removed and replaced with work samples gathered from my main school, with the occasional educational poster to fill in any gaps. All of this would be replaced by the classes work as it was generated.

Finally, I filled the lockable draws of the big old teachers' desk with desirable resources. Kids love felt pens and the bigger the pack the more they love them.

Plan an engaging educational experience

I know we are tied to a curriculum that many of us don't agree with and that many schools get very edgy if you start to move away from that, but even so there are things that you can do. More on that below.

With 8UX I only had 12 lessons {now 11} left. I also had a responsibility to the full-time teacher who would be following me so I consulted with her at every step.

We agreed something radical. For the rest of my time and then the first part of hers, the class would not be taught traditional RE. Instead I would introduce "The Utopia Project". This version is of my own devising but there are many out there. Essentially, the class arrive on a deserted island and create a new society making informed decisions on every aspect.

Eventually this led to a group of disengaged boys creating a 20-foot long montage explaining the transport systems and a group of bright students researching world religions to decide which would be the official religion of the island.

On a regular basis, groups reported back to the class, which was the governing body of the new country, and based on the information presented and the discussions that followed, decisions would be made.

This worked very well and gave the next teacher a good way into the group. It also produced a lot of fabulous work which soon decorated the room.

Raise your status in the eyes of the class
In the eyes of children new teachers, supply teachers and cover teachers are fair game. You need to make sure that they perceive you as a part of the Authority structure of the school.

There are various ways that you can do this:
1. Arrange with the management to take at least one, but ideally several, assemblies in which the kids you teach will be present. Make sure that they are good.

2. Find out when and where the Teachers In Authority are on duty and go with them. Being seen in the company of TIA's will subconsciously impact on the children's view of you.

3. If there are trips or disco's or any other fun activity, volunteer to help.

4. If you have an office, make sure that they know that. Kids are easily impressed by such things.

5. Dress to impress. I always wore a suit to work, with a different tie every week. It's not quite so straightforward for women but I'm sure that you get the point.

6. If there is an opportunity to dine with the students, you should.

Know your clients

The tendency in these difficult situations is to see the class as one big problem when, in fact, there are a series of smaller problems each of which needs a different solution.

It is never right to punish a whole class.

There will always be at least one child to whom you are doing an injustice. This child is probably the only one who wants to get on and you will lose their support by all encompassing, unfair and ineffective punishments.

In the case of 8UX the problems and solutions were as outlined below. Each class is different so you will need to apply a similar process to your problem groups.

1. *The late arrival of the whole group.*
   I should probably have learned the names of everyone in the group before I met them but complacency had made me lazy. Before the second lesson I had been to the office, obtained a photo printout of the class and memorised who was who. At the start of Lesson 2, whilst the TIA was there, I explained to the class that each child individually would complete a 50-minute lesson, whatever time they turned up. A hand went up and asked me how I would do that and I gave a few examples along the lines of;

"Well, if you, Jane, turned up on time you would go to lunch on time, whereas if you, Stephen, turned up 10 minutes late you would not leave until 1:10, by which time there would be a huge queue in the dining room."

Their faces, as they realised that I knew all of their names, were a picture.

2. *The two students who could not be saved.*
    I know this next bit sounds harsh, and it is, but given the time constraints I had few choices. If I were there full time there would have been programmes of re-integration which would have involved me spending time working with them on a one to one basis in my non-contact time whilst they were in the unit and also making contact with their families.

In this context though they had to go.

Many will agree with me when I say that there have to be lines that student behaviour cannot cross in mainstream settings. Not accepting and addressing this disrupts the learning of all, ultimately distresses and fails the child themselves and puts dreadful strains on the classroom teachers.

This is an issue which needs to be addressed at government level but in the meantime, schools must have units to which these children can be withdrawn where work can be done with them to try and make them educable in the mainstream. This may involve radically different curriculums involving the whole community.

I wrote an account of the behaviour of the twice excluded knee biter and "Stephen" and his "F**K OFF on the board incident, followed by his hiding in cupboards, throwing things out and howling and they were, to the schools' credit, managed in inclusion with work set by me from then on. There were short attempts to get them back in, with one to one support, but on each occasion the setting proved to be wrong and they were removed.

This was the case in all of their academic lessons, which is in itself food for thought.

3. *The three low ability girls with the big handbags who thought they were a "gang".*
   These were, I suspected, the source of much of the graffiti. They were up-front rude, generally uncooperative and very image conscious. Badly made-up with their "designer" bags hooked over their crooked arms.

   They had no Special Needs but they were very needy. Looking, as are we all, to be valued or even noticed. In that first lesson, they blanked me completely and swore openly in front of me but not actually at me.

After the lesson and before the next, I arranged an interview with the three of them with their Head of Year {another TIA who, as luck would have it, was an ex-student of mine}.

I described their behaviour and they blushed with embarrassment. The excellent Head of Year applied just the right amount of pressure, expressing personal disappointment and surprise and so on. I asked them one of my standard questions:

"Would you have behaved like that if your parents were actually in the room?"

The answer of course, as it almost universally is, was "No".

My follow up then is to show them my file on them, individually, topped by their name, photo and parents' mobile numbers. I then promise to call them if I am disappointed, but also if I am particularly impressed.

It is a mistake to only call parents with bad news. Many a difficult child has been turned around by a praise call, when properly earned, and the parents love it.

This policy is developed below.

Next, I asked them how I could help. They exchanged looks and then tried to explain that they were dyslexic and that this explained their behaviour. They actually weren't but that wasn't the point.

I talked about different coloured paper helping and they chose a colour each. From then on, every guidance sheet was in their chosen colour and they were never a problem again.

4. *The "Boys Own Story" Boys*
There were 4 of them. Best mates no doubt and from way back, or as way back as you can be when you are 12. Undersized, always in the same grey shirts, never quite clean. Hair that can only be described as "mousey" and "tousled". This is no reflection on the parents. These were boys who could leave for school each morning clean and tidy and 3 rough and tumbles and a tree climb later arrive at school in their trademark dishevelled state.

They were in the habit of being bored and ignored and playing. Their disruption was not deliberate, but it was continuous. To crack this problem, I had to find a way into their closed social world.

Transport was the answer. Within the Utopia Project I assigned them the role of transport planners, which then developed into being responsible for developing a town plan.

In the second lesson this was on an A3 sheet, by the end of lesson 12 it covered a 20-foot section of the wall and was astonishingly detailed. When I left we divided it up and kept a section each. They were completely absorbed by the task, took it incredibly seriously and thought through all the main issues.

5. *The "good girls" who were completely switched off.* I can't blame them. This group of 6 were well presented, well-spoken and illustrated the complex catchment area. They were typical of children of some higher-earning parents who look down on teachers and the school as a whole. They almost literally looked down their nose at me {I'm not very tall}.

In many ways, they were the easiest group to bring around. I'm in no way sexist and I don't make clichéd assumptions but given the task of designing a Zoo these animal obsessed girls really got into it. They would hop on one foot with a finger in each ear {not that I ever asked them to} for the chance to use the BIG SET OF FELT PENS {Note to the manufacturer of these sets. Please remove the pointless yellow and purple and add more blacks. The blacks always run out way before any other colours}. By the time they had finished they had drawn beautiful images of every furry animal you can think of and researched extensively about them. They found a real interest in animal welfare and conservation and a number of them became vegetarians!

6. *The Rebels*
   How do you rebel in the context of all this chaos? Simple. You refuse to join in. This group was headed by the boy who opened the door in lesson 1. He and his 2 friends, who were girls, were in the habit, which was itself disruptive, of shouting at the others for being so naughty.

   I held a meeting with them in my office and over tea and biscuits brought them into the fold. As my Lieutenants, they would help me crack the class. They were my monitors and faithful crew and as such they thrived and began to work really hard, taking on the more difficult tasks like looking into different forms of government and religion and reporting back to the class.

7. *The boy with genuine Special Needs*
   Let's call him Michael. Michael was definitely on the spectrum. Statemented but unsupported because the hours, as was common then, had been absorbed into the central budget to provide additional Teaching Assistants who only seemed to work in Maths, English and Science.

Isolated and confused, he made his way through each day somehow, producing bad pictures with semi-literate notes beneath. Having interviewed him with his lovely parents I attached him to the BIG SET OF FELT PENS and he was adopted by the Zoo group. As he relaxed they became genuinely fond of him and he also began to thrive and contribute. I also used a set of visual cue cards.

One lesson happened to fall on his birthday. After the lesson, I popped into town and bought him a card and a small Easter Egg, which I presented to him at afternoon registration. He was so happy he hugged me. After that every birthday had to be marked in a similar way. A small price to pay for an excellent caring two-way relationship with a class.

8. *Finally, the "Letter".*
   I am an absolute believer in the responsibility of parents for their child's behaviour, hence the "would you be behaving like this if your parents were standing there" comment.

   As an extension of this I wrote two formal letters, printed a class set of each and placed them on the desk at the start of the second lesson, whilst the TIA was there.

   I promised them that the parents of each child in the class would receive one or the other at the end of our 12 lessons together.

They were set out formally on headed paper, I've included only the body here. Each one would be personalised.

Letter 1

Dear Parent / Carer,

I have been teaching 8UX for the last 6 weeks.

Sadly, I have to tell you that for all of that time your child has been disruptive, rude and generally difficult.
{Insert name} has produced no work worth keeping and has actively prevented others from doing so.
I would like to meet with you as a matter of urgency to discuss where he/she learnt the words that she/he uses on a minute by minute basis and why his/her attitude to adults and learning is so appalling.

Please contact me at the school today to confirm that you have received this and to make an appointment to see me.

Sincerely

Letter 2

Dear Parent / Carer,

I have been teaching 8UX for the last 6 weeks.

I am very pleased to be able to tell you that {insert name} has been a pleasure to teach for all of that time.

{Insert name} has worked very hard and produced a large quantity of really nice work of which he / she and you can be very proud. I certainly am.

In addition, {insert name} has been polite, helpful and a pleasure to teach.

I would like to take this opportunity to thank you for being such successful parents.

I have arranged a viewing of the work of {insert name} and his / her equally successful colleagues at {insert time} on {insert date}, which I hope you will be able to attend so that we can celebrate their success together. Light refreshments will be served. Kind regards,

At the end of the 6 weeks I sent the success letters to all but the two who had been removed. They were genuinely deserved if we discounted lesson 1 and a few minor lapses over the following weeks.

The parents and children were so happy it was a real pleasure to hold the review session.

Everyday good practice
The main section above describes the sort of actions you might need to take if you find yourself in extremely difficult circumstances.

This next section is a simple list of good practice that will help you to establish outstanding behaviour for learning in more ordinary times.

First review my opening comments and empathise with your students. Accept that you need to be a full and rounded personality that is open to them and that their values and interests may not be the same as yours.

You may not agree with all of the following, and some will not be in your control, but I hope that you will find most of them useful.

1. **Dress for success.** Teachers are professionals and should dress like consultants. I know I've said this before but it is important.

2. **Be at your best.** Don't turn up for work tired and under-par because of bad choices that you have made.

3. **Be friendly whilst being clear that you are not their friend.** This may sound harsh but it isn't. You are not part of their peer group and trying to be so is a mistake. Be friendly, helpful and open but always be clear that you are an authority figure. I always spent lunch times in my room, which was always full of students. Often, they wouldn't even speak to me, but they would always be there.

4. **Be prepared.** You should never need to leave the room to get something. Every lesson should be thoroughly prepared and everything you need should be on hand. A resource area available to the students without having to ask is a good idea. They are responsible for its upkeep and tidiness.

5. **Be punctual.** There is no excuse for not being first into your room. Teachers hanging around the staffroom when the bell goes should not be doing so. Being in the teaching space first makes it yours and gives you a natural authority.

6. **Be interesting!** Teaching is a performance art. It's OK to chat and be entertaining. Share your thoughts and interests. Even if you are teaching

the deadliest of topics you can enliven the experience with varied tasks and resources. I always had a "Challenge Corner" {not my idea} with a large variety of activities, many unrelated to the curriculum but all stimulating, that the children had access to if they needed a brain break or had simply finished. This included puzzles, sudokus, chess problems, Rubik's cubes etc.

Starters needn't be topic related. Discuss current affairs, share a good Youtube video, tell them a joke, play a drama game. It's not time wasting, it's team building.

Every lesson had choices built in with charts on the wall suggesting different ways of working. I'll never forget the finger-puppet version of the Peasants Revolt! Use of a camera so the students can make instructional or dramatic films is also very stimulating. Give them the responsibility. Your role is to guide and gently push.

7. **Using the Loo.** Most school ban this during lessons. They are wrong to do so. How would you feel if you were forbidden from going during a meeting? It's outrageous. Obviously, you need to be aware of who goes and how often, especially in a large school, but you should make a professional judgement and your college

should support you in that. If only one loo is open, perhaps in a staffed medical room, a list can be kept and any patterns would soon be revealed. If a child is going in every lesson of everyday, ask why.

8. **Value their work.** I was often told that I, sadly, was the only person who displayed work by every student. If they had tried hard and done their best it went up, however poor the result was. Praise works wonders for everyone, including us as teachers. Mark every piece of work with, at least, a smiley face. If you need a break to catch up, set a long-term task or use drama.

9. **Have very high standards.** Insist on good manners and courtesy and lead by example. I always hold open the doors for students in corridors and greet everyone I know with a smile and a "Good morning". I don't push in or expect students to stand aside. I speak to the children respectfully and expect the same in return. I've even been known to carry things for them if they are struggling.

10. **Be aware of blank page syndrome.** Many students are afraid of failure and / or embarrassed by their handwriting or drawing skills. Sit down with them and get them started.

Be their secretary for a short while or allow pair work.

Provide blank outlines or frameworks. Access to lap tops or a computer suite can make a huge difference.

11. **PEP talks.** The same applies to staff and students when you ask the question, "Would you be behaving like this if a parent was in the room?" I've witnessed staff being incredibly rude to children. Raising your voice for effect is OK, ranting is not. Sarcasm has no place in the classroom. One of the children's biggest complaints about staff is that they behave differently in front of parents.

    PEP talks are the answer:

    PROXIMITY. Get close, ideally sit down next to them. Speak quietly, often invoking "the parent" question.

    EYE-CONTACT. Just that. Very powerful close up.

    PRIVACY. If you are embarrassing them in front of the class, why shouldn't they fight back? Most children will respond much more readily to a quiet private word, especially if it ends with the suggestion that you might ring home as soon as the lesson finishes and describe whatever has been going on.

12. **Be willing to ask for help.** Everyone struggles sometimes. I think Senior Staff should introduce new teachers to their classes and stay a while. Work out who your schools TIA's are and use them, if only by invoking their name.

13. **Be a part of the wider life of the school and the community.** Even if it means going to a "gig" by some awful year 11 rock band. Support trips and discos. Be seen as a positive part of the happy sides of school life.

14. **Rewards!** Golden time is a great idea, both at the end of lessons and the ends of term. Chocolates at Easter and Christmas work wonders. Be creative if your school doesn't go for this sort of approach. For example, at Christmas classes used to make vast paper chains, which they loved, with a fact written on the inside of every third loop. One year we encircled the main block.

On another occasion a Vice Principal issued an e mail banning the showing of films at the end of term that were "vaguely related to the curriculum". I replied saying, "Don't worry, the films I'm showing have got nothing at all to do with the curriculum." I didn't win that one.

And that's pretty much it.
Good luck.

Printed in Great
Britain
by Amazon